PENNY D. JOHNSTON

The Art of Goldfish Keeping

A Complete Guide to Caring for Happy, Healthy, and Vibrant Goldfish

First edition

This book was professionally typeset on Reedsy.
Find out more at reedsy.com

Contents

Introduction

Goldfish are more than just colorful decorations in a bowl—they are intelligent, responsive, and surprisingly complex creatures that can thrive for decades with the right care. The Art of Goldfish Keeping is your comprehensive guide to understanding these beloved freshwater pets, whether you're a beginner looking to set up your first tank or an experienced aquarist seeking to refine your techniques.

In this book, you'll discover the essentials of goldfish care, from choosing the right tank and filtration system to feeding, health maintenance, and creating an enriching environment. We'll explore the many fascinating varieties of goldfish, each with its own charm and needs, and provide expert insights into breeding, behavior, and common problems to avoid.

With practical tips, clear instructions, and a focus on responsible fishkeeping, this guide is designed to help you build a healthy aquatic habitat where your goldfish can live long, vibrant lives. Welcome to a journey of aquatic beauty, responsibility, and joyful companionship.

Chapter 1

Introduction to Goldfish Keeping

G oldfish are among the most iconic and beloved freshwater pets around the world. With their brilliant colors, flowing fins, and peaceful nature, goldfish offer an elegant, soothing presence in any home. But behind their simple charm lies a fascinating history and a surprisingly sophisticated level of care that can turn a beginner hobby into a lifelong passion.

A Brief History of Goldfish

Goldfish have a rich and noble heritage. Originating over a thousand years ago in ancient China, they were first domesticated from wild carp (Carassius auratus) for their unusual golden color mutations. By the Tang Dynasty (618–907 AD), goldfish were kept in ornamental ponds and water gardens by the Chinese aristocracy. This tradition spread to Japan and eventually to Europe by the 17th century, where goldfish became popular symbols of luck, prosperity, and elegance.

Today, goldfish are bred into a wide variety of shapes, colors, and sizes—each with unique characteristics that appeal to different enthusiasts.

Why Keep Goldfish at Home?

Goldfish are more than just decorative pets. They offer several benefits for hobbyists and families alike:

Low noise, high serenity: Unlike dogs or birds, goldfish are silent companions. Their gentle swimming and graceful movements can bring calm to even the busiest households.

Educational for children: Caring for goldfish can teach responsibility, patience, and respect for living creatures.

Customizable environments: Goldfish tanks can be tailored with plants, stones, and ornaments to reflect personal style while supporting the fish's needs.

Therapeutic value: Studies suggest that watching fish swim can reduce stress, lower blood pressure, and promote relaxation.

Goldfish Are Not Just "Beginner Pets"
    Despite their reputation as a first pet for children, goldfish require more than a small bowl and occasional feeding. When properly housed and cared for, goldfish can live for 10–20 years or even longer. Some have been documented to live over 40 years in ideal conditions. Their health and longevity depend on clean water, proper diet, and enough space to grow— factors often overlooked by casual owners.

Goldfish are surprisingly intelligent as well. They can recognize their owners, learn feeding schedules, and even perform simple tricks or navigate mazes. Understanding these animals

as living beings with specific needs transforms the hobby from a passive activity into an enriching experience.

The Elegant Journey Ahead
    This handbook is designed to guide you through every stage of goldfish

care—from setting up your first tank to exploring advanced techniques like breeding and aquascaping. Whether you're a curious beginner or a long-time keeper looking to deepen your knowledge, this book offers practical advice, scientific insights, and creative inspiration.

Chapter 2

Understanding Goldfish Species and Varieties

G oldfish are far more diverse than many people realize. What began as a simple golden mutation of the wild carp has evolved—through centuries of selective breeding—into a stunning array of colors, body shapes, and fin styles. Understanding these different goldfish varieties is key to choosing the right type for your home environment and level of experience.

1. Common Goldfish (Carassius auratus auratus)

Often mistaken as the "default" goldfish, the common goldfish has a long, sleek body and a single tail fin. These hardy, fast-swimming fish are well-suited for large aquariums or outdoor ponds and can grow up to 10–12 inches (25–30 cm) in length.

Ideal for: Beginners, outdoor ponds, larger tanks Pros: Very hardy, active, easy to care for
    Cons: Needs space, may outcompete slower varieties for food

1. Comet Goldfish

Comet goldfish are similar in shape to the common goldfish but are more slender and feature a longer, deeply forked tail. They are incredibly fast swimmers and are very active.

Colors: Commonly orange, red-and-white, or metallic hues Ideal for: Outdoor ponds, large tanks
  Pros: Very resilient and energetic
  Cons: Not ideal for fancy goldfish tanks due to their speed and dominance

1. Fantail Goldfish

Fantails are one of the most popular fancy goldfish, characterized by their egg-shaped body and double caudal (tail) fins that spread like a fan. They are graceful swimmers but less agile than common or comet types.

Ideal for: Indoor tanks, decorative aquariums Pros: Beautiful, classic fancy appearance
  Cons: Prone to swim bladder issues, needs stable water conditions

1. Ryukin Goldfish

Ryukins have a distinctive hump behind the head and a high, arched back. They are robust, elegant, and come in both short and long-tailed varieties. Despite their fancy look, they are relatively hardy.

Colors: Red, white, calico, chocolate, and more
  Pros: Striking appearance, good for experienced keepers Cons: May be slightly aggressive toward slower goldfish

1. Oranda Goldfish

One of the most recognizable fancy goldfish, Orandas feature a fleshy hood called a wen on their heads, giving them a unique and regal look. They are peaceful and come in a wide range of colors.

Special Care: The wen can become infected or obstruct vision Pros: Graceful, sociable, and beautiful
   Cons: Delicate head growth requires clean water and close monitoring

1. Ranchu Goldfish

Ranchus are a Japanese breed of fancy goldfish similar to Orandas but lack a dorsal fin. Their rounded back and hooded head give them a lion-like profile, earning them the nickname "King of Goldfish" in Japan.

Pros: Unique look, gentle temperament
   Cons: Very slow swimmers, best kept with other Ranchus or similar types

1. Telescope Eye Goldfish

These goldfish are named for their protruding, bulging eyes. While striking in appearance, they are poor swimmers and have limited vision, requiring a calm tank environment.

Variants: Black Moor (a popular telescope variety with velvet-black coloration) Pros: Fascinating look
   Cons: Eyes are delicate—avoid sharp tank decorations

1. Bubble Eye Goldfish

Bubble Eyes are perhaps the most delicate of all goldfish varieties. They have large fluid-filled sacs under their eyes, making them vulnerable to injury.

Tank Requirements: Soft decor, no fast or aggressive tank mates Pros: Very unique, perfect for collectors

Cons: Very fragile, not recommended for beginners

1. Pearlscale Goldfish

Known for their round bodies and raised, bead-like scales, Pearlscales look like living ornaments. Their scales are easily damaged, so handling and tank furnishings must be carefully managed.

Pros: Attractive, unusual texture
   Cons: Prone to swim bladder problems and injury

Choosing the Right Variety for You
   When selecting goldfish for your home, consider:

Experience level: Fancy varieties require more care and a stable environment.

Tank size: Larger-bodied goldfish or fast swimmers like commons and comets need more space.

Companionship: Not all goldfish types are compatible. Keep similar types together (e.g., fast with fast, fancy with fancy).
   Aesthetic preference: Do you prefer natural, sleek looks or ornamental, show-style traits? Goldfish Are All One Species—But Appear So Different
   It's important to remember that all domesticated goldfish, no matter how different they look,
   belong to the same species—Carassius auratus. Their amazing diversity is

a testament to centuries of selective breeding, and each variety has its own charm and requirements.

Chapter 3

Setting Up the Perfect Goldfish Tank

C reating a proper home for your goldfish is essential for their health, happiness, and long-term well-being. Unlike the common myth of goldfish surviving in small bowls, these elegant creatures need ample space, clean water, and a thoughtfully arranged environment. This chapter will walk you through the essential elements of setting up the perfect goldfish tank—from choosing the right size to selecting the right equipment.

1. Choosing the Right Tank Size

Bigger is always better. Goldfish produce a significant amount of waste and require a lot of oxygen. A small tank or bowl will quickly become polluted and harm your fish.

Minimum tank size per goldfish: 20 gallons (75 liters) for the first goldfish, with an additional 10 gallons (38 liters) for each additional fish.

Fancy goldfish: Slower swimmers, but still need space due to their deep bodies and sensitivity.

Common/comet goldfish: Better suited to large tanks or ponds due to their size and speed.

Tip: Long tanks are better than tall ones because they offer more surface area for oxygen exchange.

1. Essential Equipment for a Goldfish Tank

A successful goldfish setup includes the following core items:

1. Filtration System

Goldfish are messy eaters and heavy waste producers. A powerful filter is vital for keeping the water clean and toxin-free.

Use a filter rated for at least twice your tank's volume.

Choose between sponge filters (gentle, good for fancy goldfish) or hang-on-back/canister filters (great for larger setups).

1. Air Pump and Air Stone

While not mandatory, an air pump with an air stone helps oxygenate the water and create surface movement, improving overall tank health.

1. Heater (Optional)

Goldfish are cold-water fish and usually do not need a heater unless room temperature drops below 60°F (15°C). However, stable temperatures (65°F–75°F or 18°C–24°C) are ideal.

1. Lighting

Goldfish don't need strong lighting, but a well-lit tank: Encourages natural behavior
   Enhances their colors Supports live plants, if used
   LED lights are energy-efficient and customizable.

1. Substrate and Decorations Substrate

Gravel: Common choice but should be large enough not to be swallowed.
Sand: Natural-looking and safe, but can clog filters if not maintained properly.
Bare-bottom: Easier to clean, ideal for fry or quarantine tanks.
   Decorations
   Goldfish are curious and love to explore, but safety comes first:

Avoid sharp edges that could damage fins or eyes.

Use aquarium-safe materials (no metals, no painted surfaces). Provide hiding spaces (caves, driftwood) but avoid overcrowding.

1. Live or Artificial Plants

Plants provide aesthetic appeal and help maintain water quality by absorbing nitrates. Live plants: Java fern, Anubias, Hornwort, and Elodea are goldfish-safe.
   Artificial plants: Choose silk over plastic to avoid fin damage.

Note: Goldfish love to nibble plants. Choose hardy species or be prepared to replant frequently.

1. Cycling the Tank Before Adding Fish

Before introducing any fish, you must cycle the tank—a process that establishes beneficial bacteria to convert harmful ammonia into less toxic substances.

Steps to Cycle:
Add a source of ammonia (fish food, pure ammonia). Monitor water parameters using a test kit.

Wait 4–6 weeks until ammonia and nitrites drop to zero, and nitrates rise. Only then introduce goldfish.

This process prevents "new tank syndrome," which can kill fish due to toxic water.

1. Tank Placement and Setup Tips

Keep the tank away from direct sunlight (prevents algae blooms and over-heating). Ensure a strong, stable stand supports the tank weight.

Maintain consistent room temperature.

Have a secure lid or cover (goldfish can jump when startled).

1. Goldfish Tank Checklist

Before introducing your goldfish, ensure you have:
Appropriately sized tank Filter and air pump Dechlorinator for tap water Aquarium thermometer

Gravel vacuum and water testing kit Substrate and decorations

Goldfish-safe plants Properly cycled water

Creating the perfect tank environment is the cornerstone of successful goldfish keeping. With the right setup, your goldfish will have the space and conditions they need to grow, thrive, and display their full beauty.

Chapter 4

Water Quality and Maintenance

W ater quality is the lifeblood of your goldfish's health. Even with the best tank setup, poor water quality can quickly lead to illness, stress, and death. Goldfish are particularly sensitive to toxic buildups due to their high waste production. Maintaining clean, balanced water is not just a technical chore—it's an essential commitment to your goldfish's well-being.

1. Understanding the Nitrogen Cycle

The nitrogen cycle is the natural biological process that breaks down fish waste and leftover food.

Step 1: Ammonia (NH_3)
   Goldfish produce waste that breaks down into toxic ammonia.

Step 2: Nitrites (NO_2^-)
   Beneficial bacteria convert ammonia into nitrites—also toxic to fish. Step 3: Nitrates (NO_3^-)

Another group of bacteria convert nitrites into nitrates, which are much less toxic and can be controlled through water changes and live plants.

Conclusion: Establishing a complete nitrogen cycle before adding fish (as covered in Chapter 3) is critical to long-term tank health.

1. Key Water Parameters to Monitor

Keeping track of these parameters ensures a safe aquatic environment:

Parameter Ideal Range for Goldfish Ammonia 0 ppm
 Nitrites 0 ppm
 Nitrates Below 40 ppm pH 7.0–8.4
 Temperature 65–75°F (18–24°C)

Use a liquid water testing kit (preferably not strips) to regularly check these levels.

1. Dechlorination and Tap Water Treatment

Tap water contains chlorine or chloramine, both of which are toxic to fish. Before adding water to your tank:

Use a water conditioner or dechlorinator to neutralize harmful chemicals.

Let the water sit for a few minutes (after treatment) before pouring it into the tank. Condition all water used for top-offs and water changes.

1. Regular Water Changes: How and Why

Even with a good filter, waste and toxins accumulate over time. Weekly water changes are essential to remove excess nitrates and maintain clarity.

How much to change?

Weekly: 25%–40% of the total tank volume In heavily stocked tanks: up to 50%

Steps for a proper water change:

Turn off electrical equipment (heater, filter).

Use a gravel vacuum to siphon waste from the substrate. Remove 25–50% of the water.

Refill with treated water of matching temperature. Restart equipment and check everything is functioning.

Tip: Avoid changing all the water at once. Drastic changes can shock your goldfish.

1. Filter Maintenance

Filters keep your water clean but need regular attention:

Rinse filter media in used tank water (never tap water) every 2–4 weeks.

Replace filter sponges or cartridges only when necessary to preserve beneficial bacteria. Keep the filter motor and impeller clean to ensure efficient operation.

1. Managing Algae Growth

A bit of algae is natural and can even help with water quality, but excessive growth can: Block light

Reduce oxygen

Make the tank unsightly Control methods:

Avoid overfeeding (excess food feeds algae) Limit light exposure to 8–10

hours/day
  Use algae scrapers or magnetic cleaners Introduce live plants to outcompete algae

1. Troubleshooting Common Water Issues

Cloudy water: Often due to bacterial bloom—avoid overfeeding and let the cycle stabilize.

Ammonia spike: Usually caused by overfeeding or insufficient filtration. Perform a water change and stop feeding for 24 hours.

Low pH: Could indicate decaying matter—check for dead plants or uneaten food.

1. Goldfish Behavior as Water Quality Indicator Goldfish often display signs when water quality is poor:

Gasping at the surface (low oxygen) Sitting at the bottom (stress or poor water)
  Clamped fins or red streaks (ammonia/nitrite poisoning)

Never ignore sudden changes in behavior—test water immediately.

1. Developing a Maintenance Routine Consistency is key to clean water:

Daily

Observe your fish for unusual behavior Check water temperature

Weekly

Perform partial water changes Clean glass and vacuum gravel Test water parameters
   Monthly

Rinse filter media

Check equipment for wear or damage

By understanding and actively managing water quality, you ensure that your goldfish live in an environment that supports their health, vitality, and beauty. Crystal-clear, balanced water is not just a backdrop—it's the foundation of your goldfish's life.

Chapter 5

Diet and Feeding Schedule

F eeding goldfish may seem simple at first glance, but getting it right is one of the most important aspects of their care. A balanced diet not only keeps your goldfish healthy and active, but also enhances their color, supports proper growth, and prevents serious health issues like swim bladder disease and constipation.

1. Understanding Goldfish Nutritional Needs

Goldfish are omnivores, which means they eat both plant and animal-based foods. In the wild, their diet consists of algae, aquatic plants, insects, and small crustaceans. In captivity, they thrive on a combination of prepared foods and fresh supplements.

Key Nutritional Components:
Protein: Supports growth and tissue repair. Young or growing fish need more. Carbohydrates: Provide energy but should be kept moderate to prevent digestive issues. Fiber: Essential for digestion and preventing bloating.
Vitamins & minerals: Support immune function, organ health, and overall vitality.

1. Types of Goldfish Food

There are many types of food available for goldfish. A varied diet ensures they receive all necessary nutrients.

Commercial Foods:
Pellets: Ideal for larger goldfish. Sink or float varieties are available.

Flakes: Suitable for smaller or young goldfish but often lose nutrients quickly in water. Gel food: Customizable and easy to digest. Can be homemade or store-bought.
Supplemental Foods:
Vegetables: Blanched peas (shelled), spinach, lettuce, zucchini, and cucumber. Protein sources: Bloodworms, brine shrimp, daphnia (live or frozen).
Fruits: Occasionally offer soft fruits like orange slices or melon in moderation.

Tip: Blanch vegetables and remove any uneaten bits within a few hours to maintain water quality.

1. Feeding Frequency and Amount

Overfeeding is one of the most common and dangerous mistakes in goldfish care. Goldfish do not have a stomach—they digest food in their intestines, making them prone to over-eating and waste buildup.

How often to feed:
Adult goldfish: 1–2 times daily
Juveniles: 2–3 smaller meals daily How much to feed:
Only provide what they can eat in 1 to 2 minutes. Remove uneaten food promptly. General Rule: It's better to underfeed slightly than to overfeed.

1. Special Considerations for Fancy Goldfish

Fancy varieties such as Orandas, Ranchus, and Telescope Eyes are more prone to digestive issues and swim bladder disorders due to their compressed body shapes.

Prefer sinking pellets or gel food to floating flakes to prevent gulping air at the surface. Include high-fiber vegetables regularly to keep their digestive systems moving smoothly.

1. Fasting and Detox Days

Periodic fasting is beneficial for goldfish. It allows the digestive system to clear out and can help prevent bloating or constipation.

Fasting day: Once a week, skip feeding entirely.

If constipation occurs, offer shelled, blanched peas as a mild natural laxative.

1. Treats and Variety

Goldfish enjoy variety in their diet. Occasional treats can:

Stimulate natural foraging behavior Enhance coloration
    Reduce boredom in the tank

Treats should be offered sparingly—once or twice per week—and never replace the staple diet.

1. Feeding Tips for a Healthy Routine

Feed at consistent times to establish a routine.

Use feeding rings to prevent food from spreading around the tank.

Watch how each fish eats—slower goldfish may need separate feeding times to avoid competition.

Monitor water parameters after feeding, especially if trying new foods.

1. Signs of Overfeeding or Malnutrition

Watch for these red flags that may indicate dietary issues: Overfeeding Signs: Cloudy water Excess waste

Bloating or floating problems Lethargy
   Malnutrition Signs:

Faded coloration Stunted growth
   Slow recovery from illness Hollow or sunken belly

1. Homemade Food Recipes (Optional)

If you're interested in going the extra mile, you can make your own goldfish food:

Simple Goldfish Gel Food Recipe:
   1 cup of boiled vegetables (peas, spinach, carrots)

½ tsp of high-quality fish vitamins (optional) 1 packet unflavored gelatin
   Blend until smooth and pour into molds Refrigerate until set, then cut into small cubes
   Store in the fridge for up to a week or freeze for longer use.

A well-fed goldfish is a happy, active, and vibrant fish. By offering a varied and balanced diet, you support not only their physical health but also their natural behaviors and long-term vitality.

Chapter 6

Behavioral Traits of Goldfish

G oldfish are more than just ornamental swimmers; they are intelligent, curious, and social animals with a wide range of behaviors. Understanding these behaviors helps you provide better care, detect health problems early, and enjoy a deeper bond with your aquatic companions. In this chapter, we'll explore how goldfish behave in their environment and what their actions can reveal about their needs and well-being.

1. Goldfish Personalities

Contrary to common belief, goldfish have distinct personalities:

Some are bold and adventurous, eagerly exploring the tank.

Others are shy or reserved, preferring to stay near plants or corners.

Certain individuals may become particularly interactive with their keepers, swimming to the surface or front of the tank when approached.

Goldfish can even recognize the person who feeds them regularly and may learn to associate your presence with food or attention.

1. Social Behavior and Schooling

Goldfish are social animals and generally do well in groups, especially with others of similar size and temperament. Fancy goldfish, for example, should be housed with other fancies, while slim-bodied types like commons or comets thrive in larger schools.

Positive social behaviors include:

Swimming side-by-side

Gently nudging or following each other Coordinated feeding patterns
 Avoid mixing aggressive or fast-moving types with slower varieties, as this can cause stress and feeding difficulties.

1. Foraging and Food-Seeking

Goldfish are natural foragers and will constantly explore their environment in search of food. You may notice them:

Digging into gravel Picking at plants

Pushing decorations or sifting through substrate

This behavior is completely normal and helps keep them mentally stimulated. It also underscores the importance of safe, non-toxic tank decor and a clean substrate.

1. Resting and Sleeping Habits

Goldfish don't have eyelids, so they never appear to close their eyes. However, they do sleep—usually at night or during periods of low light.

Sleeping behavior includes:

Hovering near the bottom or mid-water Minimal movement
   Slightly drooping fins

As long as they respond when approached or touched, there's no cause for alarm. Sudden inactivity during the day, however, could signal stress or illness.

1. Territoriality and Aggression

Though generally peaceful, goldfish may display territorial or competitive behaviors, especially in crowded tanks or during breeding.

Signs of territorial behavior:

Chasing tank mates Nipping at fins (rare)
   Guarding a certain area or object

Provide ample space, multiple hiding spots, and avoid overcrowding to reduce these behaviors.

1. Breeding and Courtship Behavior

During mating season, especially in spring or when water temperatures rise, male goldfish may start chasing females as part of the breeding ritual.

Signs of courtship:

Persistent chasing

Nudging the female's abdomen

Tiny white tubercles on the male's gill covers and pectoral fins

This is normal and typically not aggressive unless it becomes excessive—at which point separating the fish may be necessary.

1. Curiosity and Playfulness

Goldfish love new things. Adding new plants, decor, or even a ping pong ball can capture their interest. Just make sure all items are:

Aquarium-safe

Free from sharp edges or paint Large enough not to be swallowed
   Enrichment enhances their mental health and helps prevent boredom-related stress.

1. Signs of Stress or Discomfort

Behavior is one of the first signs that something may be wrong. Watch for the following warning signs:

Behavior Possible Cause
   Gasping at the surface Low oxygen, poor water quality Rubbing or flashing Parasites or skin irritation
   Clamped fins Stress or illness

Lethargy Temperature shock, illness, or poor diet Erratic swimming Swim bladder issues or water toxins

Always test water parameters and inspect for physical symptoms if abnormal behavior is observed.

1. Goldfish and Human Interaction

Goldfish can learn to recognize their owners and may come to the surface when you approach the tank. Some can be trained to:

Eat from your hand Swim through hoops
  Perform simple tricks using food as motivation

Training builds trust and is a fun way to engage with your goldfish.

1. Understanding Behavioral Changes Over Time

As your goldfish age or adapt to their environment, their behavior may evolve. New goldfish might hide or stay still for the first few days. Older fish may slow down and rest more. Observing these trends helps you develop a strong understanding of what's "normal" for each fish, which is essential in recognizing early signs of distress.

Conclusion

Goldfish are intelligent and expressive creatures. The more time you spend observing their behavior, the more attuned you become to their needs and emotions. Whether they're playfully swimming, curiously exploring, or calmly resting, every movement is a window into their health and happiness.

Chapter 7

Goldfish Health and Common Illnesses

Healthy goldfish are active, alert, and brightly colored. But like all pets, goldfish are susceptible to various diseases—many of which can be prevented through proper care, hygiene, and early detection. In this chapter, you'll learn how to spot signs of illness, understand common goldfish diseases, and take steps to keep your aquatic companions in top condition.

1. Signs of a Healthy Goldfish

Before we explore illness, let's define what a healthy goldfish looks and acts like: Smooth, unblemished scales
   Clear, bright eyes

Active swimming with good balance Eager appetite
   Open, relaxed fins

No visible parasites or deformities

Regular observation helps you quickly notice when something seems "off."

1. Early Warning Signs of Illness

Prompt action saves lives. Watch for these signs of distress or disease: Gasping at the surface
Clamped fins (fins held tightly against the body)

Flicking or scratching against tank objects Loss of appetite
Floating problems (sinking or floating sideways) White spots, red streaks, or ulcers
Excess slime coat or cloudy eyes Lethargy or hiding
Behavioral changes often appear before physical symptoms, so don't ignore subtle signs.

1. Common Goldfish Illnesses

Here are the most frequently encountered diseases in goldfish, along with causes and treatments:

1. Ich (White Spot Disease)

Cause: Parasite Ichthyophthirius multifiliis

Symptoms: Tiny white spots like grains of salt, rubbing against objects, rapid gill movement

Treatment: Increase water temperature gradually to 78–80°F (26–27°C) and treat with Ich medication; quarantine infected fish

1. Fin Rot

Cause: Bacterial infection (often from poor water quality) Symptoms: Torn, frayed, or discolored fins with black or white edges Treatment: Improve water quality; treat with antibacterial medication

1. Swim Bladder Disease

Cause: Overfeeding, constipation, infection, or genetic deformity Symptoms: Difficulty swimming upright, floating upside down or sinking
Treatment: Fast fish for 24–48 hours; feed blanched peas; use clean, warm water

1. Dropsy

Cause: Bacterial infection, often internal organ failure Symptoms: Bloated body, raised "pinecone" scales, lethargy
Treatment: Often fatal; isolate fish, treat with antibacterial medication and salt baths

1. Velvet Disease

Cause: Parasite Oodinium

Symptoms: Dusty golden coating, scratching, lethargy Treatment: Quarantine and treat with copper-based medications

1. Anchor Worm and External Parasites Cause: Parasitic infestation

Symptoms: Visible worms attached to body, excessive rubbing, sores Treatment: Manual removal, salt dips, anti-parasitic medication

THE ART OF GOLDFISH KEEPING

1. Preventing Illness Through Proper Care

Prevention is always easier than treatment. Keep your goldfish healthy by: Maintaining excellent water quality (see Chapter 4)

Avoiding overfeeding

Quarantining new fish for 2–3 weeks before introducing them to the main tank Cleaning equipment regularly

Avoiding sudden changes in water temperature or pH Providing a balanced diet

A stress-free environment boosts the immune system and reduces the chance of disease.

1. The Role of Aquarium Salt

Aquarium salt (sodium chloride) can be helpful in treating mild infections and boosting slime coat production.

Safe usage:

1 tablespoon per 5 gallons (19 liters) for minor issues Gradually dissolve in tank water before adding

Don't use with scaleless fish or live plants

Avoid using salt continuously—it's best used for short treatments or during quarantine.

1. Isolation and Quarantine Tanks

A separate quarantine tank is highly recommended for: Treating sick fish without medicating the entire tank

Monitoring new arrivals before introducing them to the main tank Reducing the spread of contagious diseases

A basic quarantine tank should include:

Sponge filter or air stone Heater (if needed) Hiding spots

No substrate (for easier cleaning)

1. When to Seek Professional Help

If symptoms persist or worsen despite your efforts, consider:

Consulting a veterinarian with aquatic experience Bringing a water sample to a pet store for testing

Taking high-resolution photos or videos to share with online goldfish forums Quick diagnosis is essential—many illnesses are treatable if caught early.

1. Keeping a Health Log

Tracking health events helps you detect patterns. Note:

Date of symptoms Appearance changes Medications used Water test results Recovery or outcome

Over time, this becomes an invaluable tool in managing fish health, especially in tanks with multiple fish.

Conclusion

Goldfish can live long, healthy lives—often 10 to 20 years or more—when cared for properly. Regular monitoring, clean water, a balanced diet, and prompt action at the first sign of illness are the best defenses against disease.

Chapter 8

Breeding Goldfish at Home

B reeding goldfish at home is a fascinating and rewarding aspect of goldfish keeping. It not only allows you to witness the full life cycle of these elegant creatures but also gives you the opportunity to raise healthy, well-socialized young. However, successful breeding requires preparation, the right environment, and an understanding of the goldfish reproductive process.

1. Understanding Goldfish Reproduction

Goldfish are egg layers and external fertilization breeders. Males chase females during spawning and fertilize the eggs as they are laid. Breeding usually occurs in the spring when water temperatures rise, mimicking seasonal changes in nature.

Breeding Age
  Goldfish become sexually mature at around 1–2 years of age, although optimal breeding often occurs when they are 2–4 years old.

Breeding Season
  In natural conditions, goldfish breed during spring when water temper-

atures rise to 68–74°F (20–23°C). In aquariums, you can simulate this by gradually increasing temperature and providing a proper light cycle.

1. Identifying Males and Females

Before breeding, it's important to distinguish between male and female goldfish: Males:

Develop tiny white tubercles (breeding stars) on their gill covers and pectoral fins Chase females persistently during spawning

Appear slimmer when viewed from above Females:

Appear fuller or rounder in the abdomen, especially when filled with eggs

Display less aggressive behavior

May release eggs when gently pressed (only if necessary for observation)

1. Setting Up a Breeding Tank

To avoid stress and maximize survival rates, it's ideal to use a separate breeding tank.

Tank Specifications:

Size: 20–30 gallons (75–115 liters) or larger Temperature: 68–74°F (20–23°C)

Substrate: Bare-bottom tank is preferred for easy cleaning Filtration: Sponge filter (gentle to protect eggs and fry)

Lighting: Simulate day-night cycle (12 hours light, 12 hours dark)

Spawning Materials:

Use spawning mops, fine-leaf plants (live or artificial), or soft brushes where eggs can be deposited.

Eggs are sticky and will adhere to these materials.

1. Inducing Spawning To encourage spawning:

Separate males and females for about 2 weeks.

Feed both sexes a high-protein diet (live or frozen food such as brine shrimp, bloodworms). Gradually raise water temperature by a few degrees daily.
   Reintroduce males and females in the early morning when lighting begins.

Spawning often begins with males chasing females and can last several hours. The female lays hundreds to thousands of eggs.

1. Post-Spawning Care Once spawning is complete:

Remove adult goldfish from the tank to prevent them from eating the eggs. Use an antifungal treatment like methylene blue to reduce egg loss.
   Maintain clean water and gentle aeration.

1. Hatching the Eggs

Goldfish eggs hatch in 3–7 days depending on water temperature. Healthy eggs: Clear or amber in color
   Unfertilized eggs: Turn white and should be removed to prevent fungus spread

Newly hatched fry (called "wigglers") will remain attached to surfaces for 2–3 days while absorbing their yolk sacs.

1. Caring for Goldfish Fry

Once fry become free-swimming (around day 4–5), begin feeding:

Feeding Schedule:
   Days 1–5: Infusoria or commercial liquid fry food

After day 5: Baby brine shrimp, microworms, finely crushed flake or fry-specific food

Feed small amounts 3–5 times daily, ensuring good water quality with regular water changes.

Growth Tips:
   Maintain warm, clean water

Avoid overcrowding by thinning out or using multiple tanks

Separate larger fry from smaller ones to prevent bullying or cannibalism

1. Growth and Development Milestones Week 2–4: Fry begin to resemble tiny goldfish

Week 4–6: Begin developing pigment and body shape Week 8+: Cull for deformities (optional in selective breeding)
   3 Months: Juveniles ready for larger tanks or to join the community

1. Ethical Considerations and Culling

Responsible breeding includes selecting healthy parents and culling fry that exhibit deformities, swim bladder issues, or extreme stunting. Culling can be controversial, but it's often done to ensure the health and quality of the remaining fish—especially in selective breeding programs.

If you're not breeding for show or commercial purposes, allow fry to grow naturally and rehome surplus juveniles responsibly.

1. The Joy of Raising Goldfish from Eggs

Watching fry grow into healthy adult goldfish is a truly fulfilling experience. Each stage—from the tiny wiggler to the graceful swimmer—offers insights into the resilience and beauty of life. While breeding goldfish at home requires planning, care, and patience, the results can be deeply rewarding both emotionally and visually.

Chapter 9

Feeding Your Goldfish the Right Way

Feeding your goldfish might seem like a simple task—sprinkle some food and walk away. However, a thoughtful and well-balanced diet is one of the most important elements in maintaining your goldfish's health, vitality, and longevity. In this chapter, we explore what goldfish need nutritionally, how often to feed them, what to avoid, and how their diet should evolve through different life stages.

1. Understanding Goldfish Digestion

Goldfish are omnivores and have no stomach. Instead, they rely on a long intestinal tract that continuously processes food. This means:

They need frequent, small meals rather than infrequent large ones.

Overfeeding can lead to digestive issues, water pollution, and swim bladder disorders.

1. Core Nutritional Needs A goldfish diet should be:

THE ART OF GOLDFISH KEEPING

High in fiber (for digestive health)

Balanced in protein (especially for young and growing fish) Low in fat (excess fat can cause organ damage)

Enriched with vitamins (A, C, D, E for immune health, growth, and coloration)

1. Types of Goldfish Food

Here's a breakdown of popular food types and their pros and cons:

Pellets (Sinking or Floating)
   Pros: Nutritionally balanced, widely available

Cons: Floating pellets may cause air ingestion (linked to swim bladder issues)

Tip: Soak pellets in tank water for a few seconds before feeding to soften them and prevent choking.

Flake Food
   Pros: Easy to use, inexpensive
   Cons: Loses nutrients quickly when exposed to air or light; not suitable for larger goldfish Gel Food
   Pros: Easy to digest, customizable, ideal for fancy varieties Cons: Requires preparation and refrigeration
   Fresh Vegetables
   Examples: Blanched peas (deshelled), spinach, zucchini, cucumber, kale Pros: High in fiber, good for digestion
   Tip: Feed 2–3 times a week to aid bowel health and prevent constipation.

Live or Frozen Foods
   Examples: Bloodworms, brine shrimp, daphnia, tubifex worms Pros: High

protein content, promotes growth and conditioning Cons: Risk of parasites if not properly prepared or sourced

1. Feeding Schedule by Age

Life Stage Feeding Frequency Recommended Food Types
   Fry (0–8 weeks) 3–5 times daily Infusoria, baby brine shrimp, powdered food Juveniles 2–3 times daily Pellets, flakes, vegetables, frozen foods
   Adults 1–2 times daily Pellets, gel food, veggies, live/frozen food
   Breeding Season 2–3 times daily (small meals) High-protein foods, vegetables

1. Portion Control: How Much is Enough?

A general rule is to feed only what your goldfish can consume in under 2 minutes, once or twice per day. Overfeeding leads to:

Poor water quality due to decaying uneaten food Obesity and fatty liver disease
   Swim bladder problems (especially in fancy goldfish)

If your fish appear bloated or stop swimming normally, withhold food for a day or switch to vegetables like peas to aid digestion.

1. Seasonal Feeding Adjustments

Goldfish metabolism is temperature-dependent:

Cold Water (<55°F / <13°C): Metabolism slows. Feed less often or stop altogether. Moderate Water (65–75°F / 18–24°C): Optimal feeding time. Growth and breeding occur.

Warm Water (>80°F / >27°C): Feed small, easily digestible meals. Monitor for signs of stress.

1. Supplements and Color Enhancers

For vibrant colors and optimal health, consider occasional additions like: Spirulina: Boosts immune system and enhances orange/red coloration Carotenoids: Natural pigments found in foods like krill and shrimp Vitamin-rich gel foods: Help with healing and stress resistance

Avoid overusing color-enhancing foods, especially artificial ones, which may damage liver health over time.

1. Signs of a Properly Fed Goldfish Healthy goldfish show the following signs:

Bright, vibrant colors

Smooth, continuous swimming patterns Clear eyes and strong fin posture Regular, firm waste

If your fish are constantly foraging or showing aggression at feeding time, consider adjusting the quantity or frequency of meals.

1. Common Feeding Mistakes

Overfeeding: Most common and most dangerous mistake

Feeding only flakes: Lacks diversity and may cause nutritional gaps Not adjusting diet by season or age

Ignoring floating food risks: Leads to buoyancy issues

Neglecting fasting days: One day of fasting per week promotes gut health

1. Conclusion: Feeding Is a Daily Bonding Ritual

Feeding is more than nourishment—it's an opportunity to observe, bond, and monitor your goldfish's health and behavior. A varied, nutrient-rich, and mindful feeding routine ensures your goldfish not only survives but thrives with elegance and vitality.

Chapter 10

Understanding Goldfish Behavior and Communication

G oldfish are more than colorful ornaments gliding through water—they are intelligent, social creatures that express themselves in subtle yet meaningful ways. By learning to interpret goldfish behavior, you can better monitor their health, comfort, and even mood, allowing for timely intervention and a stronger bond between you and your aquatic companions.

1. Goldfish Intelligence and Awareness Goldfish have demonstrated the ability to:

Recognize their owners Respond to feeding routines
   Learn simple tricks (like swimming through hoops or pushing objects) Remember routines and locations within their tank
   This level of awareness means that goldfish can form associations and even express excitement or anxiety depending on the environment and care they receive.

1. Common Goldfish Behaviors and Their Meanings Behavior Possible

Meaning

Active swimming and exploring Healthy, content goldfish

Hovering near the surface Anticipating food; possibly gasping due to low oxygen

Darting or erratic swimming Stress, poor water quality, or external irritation (such as parasites)

Rubbing against tank décor Potential parasite infestation (flashing behavior)

Clamped fins Illness, poor water conditions, or stress

Lethargy or bottom-sitting Fatigue, cold water, illness, or swim bladder disorder Floating upside down Likely swim bladder issue—often linked to diet, infection, or genetics

Chasing tank mates Breeding behavior (especially males chasing females) or territorial stress if space is limited

Rapid gill movement Low oxygen levels, ammonia/nitrite poisoning, or gill parasites

1. Breeding-Related Behavior

During mating season (usually spring/summer or after a temperature shift), goldfish may display:

Chasing and nudging: Males will pursue females, nudging their bellies to stimulate egg release.

White breeding tubercles: Males often develop small white bumps on their gill covers and pectoral fins.

Egg-laying: Females will scatter eggs among plants or décor; males follow to fertilize them.

This is a normal process but can become stressful if persistent or aggressive—especially in small tanks.

1. Signs of Social Interaction

Goldfish are not solitary by nature. They often form loose schools or swim in groups. In a community setup:

Schooling: Indicates a peaceful, stress-free environment.

Nudging or swimming side by side: May signal curiosity or affection.

Territorial behavior: Can happen in crowded tanks or between incompatible breeds. To promote healthy interactions, provide adequate space and hiding spots.

1. Understanding Goldfish Vocalization (Sort Of)

Goldfish don't vocalize in the traditional sense, but they do "communicate" using: Body language (swimming posture, fin movement)
   Tank positioning (surface vs. bottom, open vs. hiding) Feeding responses (excitement, jumping)
   Observing these patterns daily helps you understand what is normal and when something might be wrong.

1. Recognizing Stress in Goldfish

Stress in goldfish is often subtle. Common causes include:

Poor water quality Overcrowding Aggressive tank mates
   Sudden temperature changes Improper diet

Signs of stress:

Pale coloration Erratic swimming Appetite loss
Excessive hiding or lethargy

Identifying and correcting stressors early improves overall well-being and prevents disease outbreaks.

1. Enhancing Goldfish Behavior Through Enrichment

Mental stimulation is essential, even for fish. Here's how to enrich their environment: Varied décor and tunnels: Encourages exploration
Floating toys or feeding rings: Adds challenge and engagement

Training exercises: Using food as positive reinforcement, goldfish can be trained to follow a finger or perform simple tasks

Live plants: Offers natural foraging and shelter

A well-stimulated goldfish is more alert, interactive, and emotionally balanced.

1. Monitoring for Illness Through Behavior

Behavioral changes are often the first sign something is wrong. If your goldfish: Stops eating suddenly
Becomes unusually aggressive Develops spasmodic movements Avoids light or tank mates

...then it may be time to test water parameters or consult an aquatic vet. Prevention is always better than cure, and early detection often saves lives.

1. Bonding with Your Goldfish

While goldfish won't cuddle or purr, they do recognize their caregivers. Signs of bonding include:

Swimming toward you during feeding Following your finger along the glass Not hiding when you approach
   Consistent, gentle interactions and routine feeding help build trust and familiarity.

1. Conclusion: Learn Their Language

Goldfish have a language all their own—rooted in movement, posture, and presence. By observing and responding to their behavior, you become more than just a caretaker; you become an attentive companion. This deeper understanding strengthens your connection and ensures your goldfish thrive in their aquatic world.

Chapter 11

Common Goldfish Diseases and Treatments

E ven with the best care, goldfish can sometimes fall ill. Recognizing the early signs of disease and knowing how to respond can make the difference between recovery and loss. This chapter outlines the most common goldfish ailments, their causes, symptoms, and practical treatment methods to help you maintain a healthy aquarium.

1. Why Goldfish Get Sick

Goldfish illnesses often stem from:

Poor water quality (ammonia, nitrite spikes, low oxygen) Overcrowding

Stress (from sudden changes in temperature, aggressive tank mates, etc.) Contaminated food or unclean equipment
    Parasites, bacteria, or fungal infections

Maintaining excellent tank hygiene and routine care minimizes the risk of disease.

1. Common Goldfish Diseases
2. Ich (White Spot Disease)

Cause: Ichthyophthirius multifiliis, a parasitic protozoa

Symptoms: Tiny white spots like grains of salt on the body and fins, rubbing against objects, clamped fins, rapid breathing

Treatment:

Raise water temperature gradually to 78–80°F (25–27°C) Add aquarium salt (as directed)
    Use over-the-counter ich medications containing formalin, malachite green, or copper

1. Fin Rot

Cause: Bacterial infection (often due to poor water conditions) Symptoms: Fraying, ragged fins, redness at fin edges, sluggish behavior Treatment:
    Improve water quality with frequent water changes

Use antibacterial medications (e.g., API Melafix or aquarium-specific antibiotics)

Isolate infected fish if necessary

1. Swim Bladder Disorder

Cause: Overfeeding, gulping air while eating, constipation, infection, or physical deformity Symptoms: Difficulty swimming, floating upside down, sinking to the bottom

Treatment:

Fast the fish for 24–48 hours

Feed peeled, cooked peas to relieve constipation Reduce water current and keep the fish in shallow water

Avoid floating pellets—use sinking food

1. Dropsy

Cause: Internal bacterial infection

Symptoms: Swollen belly, raised scales (pinecone appearance), lethargy
Treatment:
   Very difficult to treat—often fatal Isolate the fish immediately
   Use antibacterial treatments (kanamycin, Maracyn 2)

Improve water conditions to prevent spread

1. Fungal Infections

Cause: Secondary infection from injury or poor tank hygiene Symptoms: Cotton-like white or gray patches on skin or fins Treatment:
   Apply antifungal medications (methylene blue, Pimafix) Remove infected tissue if advised by a vet
   Ensure excellent water quality and reduce stress

1. Anchor Worms and External Parasites

Cause: Parasites, often introduced via new plants or fish

Symptoms: Worm-like protrusions on the skin, red sores, flashing behavior
Treatment:
   Manually remove worms with tweezers under sedation (in severe cases)
Use anti-parasitic medications (like Dimilin or potassium permanganate)
Quarantine new additions to prevent spread

1. General Disease Prevention Tips

Maintain stable water parameters: Regularly test for ammonia, nitrites, nitrates, and pH. Perform weekly water changes (25–50% depending on tank size).

Use a high-quality filter and clean it monthly without disturbing beneficial bacteria. Avoid overfeeding: Feed small amounts once or twice daily.
   Quarantine new fish or plants for at least two weeks.

Avoid sudden temperature changes and stress factors like overcrowding or aggression. Clean tank decorations and vacuum substrate regularly to remove waste and uneaten food.

1. First Aid: Creating a Hospital Tank

A hospital tank (or quarantine tank) is a smaller, bare-bottomed aquarium used to isolate sick or injured fish. Key features include:

Volume: 5–20 gallons Heater (if needed) Sponge filter or air stone
   No gravel or décor (easier to clean) Dim lighting and quiet environment
   This setup makes treatment easier, prevents spreading disease to healthy fish, and allows closer observation.

1. When to Consult an Aquatic Vet

While many goldfish ailments can be treated at home, some cases require expert intervention. Contact a veterinarian if:

The fish shows signs of chronic illness despite treatment You're unsure of the disease or proper medication Multiple fish in the tank are affected
There are signs of internal infection or organ failure

Veterinary professionals with aquatic experience can offer diagnosis, medication, and advanced care like fluid injections or surgery.

1. The Importance of Observation

Early detection saves lives. Make it a daily habit to: Observe your goldfish's behavior and appearance

Check for changes in appetite, coloration, and swimming Test your water parameters weekly
Keep a logbook if managing multiple fish or issues

1. Building a Healthy Immune System Goldfish thrive when they have:

A varied, nutrient-rich diet (including fresh veggies and quality pellets) Clean, oxygen-rich water
Low-stress environments

Consistent lighting and temperature cycles
A strong immune system helps goldfish fight off disease before it takes hold.
Conclusion: Prevention Is Better Than Cure

Understanding goldfish diseases and how to treat them is essential to being a responsible owner. But even more important is preventing illness through good care practices. Clean water, proper nutrition, and attentive observation form the foundation of long-term health for your aquatic companions.

Chapter 12

Goldfish Feeding and Nutrition

Feeding your goldfish may seem simple at first glance, but providing the right diet is essential for their health, coloration, growth, and lifespan. A well-balanced diet not only supports physical well-being but also boosts immunity, enhances energy levels, and prevents common issues like swim bladder disorders and bloating.

1. Understanding Goldfish Diet Needs

Goldfish are omnivorous and naturally feed on a variety of food sources in the wild, including algae, plant matter, small insects, and crustaceans. In captivity, replicating this diverse diet helps maintain a healthy digestive system and supports all-around vitality.

Key nutritional needs include:

Proteins: Essential for growth and tissue repair Carbohydrates: Provide energy (should be limited) Fats: Needed in small amounts for metabolic function
   Vitamins and minerals: Boost immunity, enhance coloration, and maintain bone and scale health

Fiber: Helps digestion and prevents constipation

1. Types of Goldfish Food
2. Flakes

Readily available and easy to use Float on the water surface
  Can lose nutritional value quickly once exposed to air

May cause goldfish to gulp air, leading to buoyancy issues

1. Pellets

Come in floating or sinking varieties

Sinking pellets are generally preferred to reduce air intake

Offer balanced nutrients but should be soaked before feeding to prevent bloating

1. Gel Food

Soft, moist, and highly digestible

Can be homemade or purchased pre-made

Ideal for fancy goldfish that are prone to digestive issues

1. Frozen and Live Foods

Bloodworms, daphnia, brine shrimp, tubifex worms Provide protein and enrichment

Feed occasionally as treats—not staples

Always rinse live foods before use to avoid introducing parasites

1. Fresh Vegetables

Blanched peas (shelled), spinach, lettuce, zucchini, carrots Great source of fiber

Helps prevent constipation and swim bladder problems

1. Feeding Schedule and Portion Control

Overfeeding is a leading cause of water pollution and goldfish health issues. Feeding tips:

Feed once or twice a day

Offer only what they can consume in 2–3 minutes Remove uneaten food promptly

Fast your goldfish once a week to give their digestive systems a break

Young goldfish may require more frequent feeding, while adults can thrive with a single feeding per day.

1. Homemade Goldfish Food

You can prepare nutritious gel or paste foods at home using ingredients like: Blended peas, carrots, and spinach

Gelatin (as a binder)

Fish fillets or shrimp for protein

Vitamins or spirulina for color enhancement

Homemade food ensures quality control and can be tailored to your goldfish's dietary needs.

1. Special Dietary Needs of Fancy Goldfish

Fancy varieties (e.g., Orandas, Ryukins, Ranchus) are more prone to buoyancy issues due to their compressed body shapes. To reduce the risk:

Prefer sinking pellets or gel food Avoid dry flakes or floating pellets
Incorporate fibrous vegetables like peas several times a week

1. Signs of Poor Nutrition

Watch for these indicators of dietary imbalance:

Faded or dull coloration Lethargy or hyperactivity
Poor growth or bloated appearance Floating or sinking issues
Frayed fins or frequent illness

Adjusting the diet and improving water quality usually corrects these issues.

1. Treats and Enrichment Feeding

In addition to regular meals, occasional treats offer both stimulation and extra nutrition: Live or frozen brine shrimp
Chopped earthworms Spirulina flakes

Blanched cucumber or zucchini slices

These enrichments encourage natural foraging behavior and reduce boredom.

1. Water Quality and Feeding

Leftover food quickly decays and releases toxins like ammonia, which compromise goldfish health. Always:

Use a gravel vacuum to remove waste Avoid overfeeding
  Clean filters regularly

Test water parameters weekly

1. Seasonal Feeding Tips

Goldfish metabolism is affected by water temperature:

In colder months (<60°F / 15°C): Slow their metabolism, feed less, and avoid high-protein foods

In warmer months: Increase feeding frequency and use protein-rich foods to support growth and energy

Outdoor pond goldfish may stop eating entirely during winter hibernation. Do not feed if temperatures fall below 50°F (10°C).

Conclusion: Feed for Health, Not Just Hunger
  Feeding your goldfish isn't just a task—it's a daily opportunity to connect, observe, and ensure their well-being. A thoughtful, well-planned diet leads to vibrant colors, energetic behavior, and a longer, healthier life.

Chapter 13

Goldfish Breeding at Home

B reeding goldfish can be an exciting and rewarding part of goldfish keeping. Whether you're doing it out of curiosity or to raise your own healthy stock, understanding the process of goldfish reproduction is essential. With the right conditions and care, even beginners can successfully breed goldfish in a home aquarium or pond.

1. Understanding Goldfish Reproduction

Goldfish are egg-layers that breed through external fertilization. A mature female releases eggs, and a male fertilizes them by spraying milt (sperm) over the eggs. Successful breeding requires healthy, mature fish, clean water, proper nutrition, and the right environmental cues.

1. Age and Breeding Readiness

Goldfish typically reach sexual maturity at around 8–12 months, although ideal breeding age is usually 1.5 to 2 years or older for better results. Mature goldfish should be:

Well-fed and healthy

Maintained in a stable, stress-free environment

Free from deformities or genetic defects (especially if breeding fancy varieties)

1. Sexing Your Goldfish

Distinguishing between males and females can be tricky, especially outside breeding season. Look for these signs:

Males:

Develop breeding tubercles (white spots) on gill covers and pectoral fins during breeding season

Tend to be slimmer and more streamlined Chase females during spawning
Females:
  Appear rounder or fuller-bodied when filled with eggs

Have a more convex, slightly protruding vent (egg-opening)

1. Preparing for Breeding
2. Separate Breeding Tank

Set up a breeding tank (20–40 gallons minimum) to provide a controlled environment. It should have:

Soft sponge filter (to protect eggs and fry)

Heater (optional but useful for triggering breeding with temperature change)

Live or artificial spawning mops/plants for egg attachment
A secure, calm environment with low water flow

1. Conditioning the Breeders

Feed both sexes high-quality food for 2–4 weeks before breeding

Include live or frozen foods (brine shrimp, bloodworms) to enhance conditioning

1. Triggering Spawning

Goldfish breeding is stimulated by environmental changes that mimic spring:
Gradually raise water temperature from 60°F (15°C) to 74–78°F (23–26°C)
Increase daylight hours using aquarium lights (12–14 hours/day)
Perform partial water changes with slightly warmer water

Spawning usually occurs early in the morning, often following these changes.

1. The Spawning Process During spawning:

Males will chase and nudge the female, often aggressively Females release hundreds to thousands of eggs

Males release milt to fertilize them

The process may last several hours. After spawning:

Immediately remove adult goldfish to prevent them from eating the eggs

1. Caring for Goldfish Eggs

Goldfish eggs are sticky and will adhere to plants or spawning mops Fertilized eggs are clear to slightly golden
Unfertilized or fungus-infected eggs turn white and should be removed

Maintain water temperature at 74–78°F (23–26°C). Add a few drops of methylene blue to prevent fungal growth, if needed.

1. Hatching and Fry Care

Eggs hatch in about 4–7 days, depending on temperature. Fry remain attached to surfaces for a day or two, absorbing their yolk sacs before becoming free-swimming.

At this stage:

Begin feeding infusoria, then baby brine shrimp, microworms, or finely crushed flakes Keep water clean with frequent small water changes
Use sponge filters to avoid sucking up delicate fry

1. Growing Out the Fry As the fry grow:

Sort them by size to prevent cannibalism

Gradually introduce larger foods like crushed pellets

Cull deformed or unhealthy fry (especially in fancy breeds)

By 8–12 weeks, you'll start to see distinct body shapes and colors.

1. Challenges in Breeding

While breeding can be enjoyable, it's not without difficulties: Not all eggs will hatch or survive
    Some fancy goldfish may have trouble breeding naturally

Crowding, poor genetics, and lack of care can lead to weak offspring

Patience, observation, and proper planning are key to success.

Conclusion: From Breeding to Beauty
    Breeding goldfish at home allows you to witness the full life cycle of these beautiful creatures. It deepens your understanding and appreciation for their needs and behavior while giving you the joy of raising your own unique goldfish from egg to adult.

Chapter 14

Goldfish Behavior and Social Interaction

U nderstanding the behavior and social dynamics of goldfish is key to maintaining a peaceful, healthy aquarium. Goldfish are more than just ornamental fish—they are intelligent, curious, and surprisingly social animals. By learning their behavioral patterns and interaction styles, you can better recognize signs of health, stress, and even emotion in your aquatic companions.

1. Natural Behavior in Captivity

In the wild, goldfish ancestors lived in slow-moving freshwater bodies like ponds and rivers. In captivity, they display similar behaviors adapted to their enclosed environments:

Foraging: Goldfish spend much of their day rooting around for food. They will sift through gravel, nibble on plants, and explore decorations for edible material.

Swimming Patterns: Healthy goldfish swim gracefully and evenly. They often explore their surroundings and swim to the surface when sensing movement or light, anticipating food.

Resting: Goldfish do not sleep in the traditional sense but rest motionlessly, usually at the bottom or mid-levels of the tank, often with slightly drooping fins.

1. Social Hierarchy and Group Living

Goldfish are not territorial but can establish a subtle social structure, especially in groups:

Dominance: Larger or more confident goldfish may assert dominance by getting first access to food or gently nudging others.

Shoaling: While not true schooling fish, goldfish do enjoy company. They tend to stay close to one another and interact through movement and body positioning.

Chasing: During breeding or playful interactions, goldfish may chase each other. Constant or aggressive chasing, however, may indicate stress or imbalance.

Tip: Keep goldfish in compatible groups. Fancy goldfish should generally be housed with other fancies to avoid competition from faster, more streamlined types.

1. Communication Methods

Goldfish communicate primarily through:

Body language: Posture, swimming speed, and fin position signal mood and health. Clamped fins, erratic swimming, or floating upside down suggest illness or stress.

Color changes: Temporary changes in coloration may result from stress, temperature shifts, or mood. Gradual fading may indicate aging, poor diet, or illness.

Behavioral cues: Rubbing against objects (flashing), excessive hiding, or loss of appetite can signal discomfort or infection.

1. Personality Traits in Goldfish

Just like cats and dogs, goldfish have distinct personalities. Some are bold and always at the front of the tank, while others are shy and reserved. With time and observation, you can learn the unique habits and quirks of each fish:

Inquisitive fish: Often follow your finger, investigate new decorations, or quickly recognize feeding times.

Timid fish: May take time to adjust to new tank mates or environments and prefer hiding spaces.

Creating a calm, enriched tank helps all types of personalities thrive.

1. Signs of Stress or Aggression

Recognizing unusual behavior can help you catch problems early:

Behavior Possible Cause

Hiding excessively New environment, bullying, or illness Gasping at the surface Poor water quality or low oxygen Clamped fins Stress, poor water, or disease

Rubbing against objects Parasites or skin irritation Nipping or fin damageOvercrowding, aggression, or breeding

Solution: Check water quality, ensure proper tank size, and observe group dynamics. Isolating aggressive fish temporarily can help restore harmony.

1. Enriching Social and Environmental Lives

To stimulate healthy behaviors:

Add variety: Change decorations occasionally or rotate hiding places to spark exploration. Feed interactively: Vary food type and placement to encourage natural foraging.

Offer social interaction: Regular observation and gentle movement outside the tank can help fish recognize and respond to you.

1. Goldfish and Human Bonding

Goldfish may not bond in the same way dogs do, but they do develop recognition: They can learn your feeding schedule and anticipate your presence.

They may come to the surface or follow your finger, especially if you consistently interact during feeding times.

Some owners even teach goldfish to perform simple tricks using food as a reward. Conclusion: Behavior as a Window to Well-Being

Goldfish behavior reflects their environment, health, and relationships. When you understand

what's "normal" for your fish, you'll be better equipped to detect when something's off—and respond appropriately. Observing their personalities and interactions adds a rewarding emotional dimension to the hobby and enhances your connection to these graceful aquatic companions.

Chapter 15

Common Health Issues and Treatments

E ven with the best care, goldfish can occasionally suffer from illness. As a responsible keeper, being able to identify early symptoms and administer prompt treatment is essential for your goldfish's well-being. Many goldfish ailments stem from environmental issues, making prevention just as important as treatment.

1. General Signs of Illness in Goldfish

Before diving into specific diseases, here are common signs that your goldfish may be unwell:

Loss of appetite

Lethargy or unusual resting Clamped fins
  Erratic or sluggish swimming Gasping at the surface
  Rubbing against objects (flashing) Visible wounds or growths Discoloration or fading color
  Tip: Early observation and water testing are crucial. Often, water quality is the root of health problems.

1. Common Goldfish Diseases and Treatments
2. Ich (White Spot Disease)

Symptoms: Tiny white dots on fins and body, scratching on surfaces, rapid gill movement. Cause: Parasitic protozoan Ichthyophthirius multifiliis.
Treatment:

Raise water temperature slowly to 78–80°F (if safe for your species). Use commercial Ich treatments (malachite green or formalin-based). Add aquarium salt as directed to reduce stress.

1. Fin Rot

Symptoms: Fraying, discoloration, or decaying fins.

Cause: Bacterial infection, often following injury or poor water quality. Treatment:
Improve water quality through partial water changes.

Treat with antibacterial medication (e.g., Maracyn or API Fin & Body Cure). Remove sharp or rough tank decorations.

1. Swim Bladder Disorder

Symptoms: Floating upside down, sinking, trouble swimming upright. Cause: Overfeeding, constipation, or bacterial infection.
Treatment:

Fast the goldfish for 24–48 hours.

Feed cooked, peeled peas to relieve constipation. Keep water temperature stable.

For persistent cases, use antibacterial treatment.

1. Fungal Infections

Symptoms: Cotton-like growths on body or fins.

Cause: Fungi growing on open wounds or in poor water. Treatment: Quarantine affected fish.

Use antifungal medications (e.g., methylene blue). Improve water cleanliness.

1. Anchor Worm or External Parasites

Symptoms: Thread-like worms attached to skin, inflammation, flashing.
Cause: Parasites introduced from new fish or plants.
Treatment:

Manually remove with tweezers under sedation (only for experienced keepers). Treat tank with anti-parasitic medication like Dimilin.
Quarantine new additions before adding them to the main tank.

1. Dropsy

Symptoms: Swollen belly, raised scales (pinecone effect), lethargy.

Cause: Internal bacterial infection, often from organ failure or poor conditions. Treatment:

Isolate affected fish immediately. Treat with antibacterial medication.
Often fatal—focus on prevention with clean water and balanced diet.

1. Prevention Is the Best Medicine

Many goldfish illnesses can be prevented with proper husbandry. Follow these preventive measures:

Regular Water Changes: Perform weekly partial water changes (25–50%).

Test Water Quality: Use test kits to monitor ammonia, nitrite, nitrate, pH, and temperature.

Quarantine New Additions: Isolate new fish for 2–4 weeks before adding them to your main tank.

Avoid Overcrowding: Allow 20–30 gallons per adult goldfish.

Feed Responsibly: Avoid overfeeding. Provide a balanced diet with variety. Clean Tank Equipment: Rinse filters and remove waste buildup regularly.

1. Emergency Care and When to Seek Help Some situations require urgent intervention:

Symptom Action
Fish gasping, all at surface Check oxygen and ammonia levels immediately
Rapid color fading or red streaks Test water; perform partial change; monitor closely Multiple deaths in short time Suspect poisoning or contagious outbreak
Bloated fish with pinecone scales Isolate; treat with antibiotics; prognosis guarded

When in doubt: Consult a veterinarian with aquatic experience. Many regions now have vets who specialize in fish care or exotics.

1. Stocking a Fish First Aid Kit

Keep the following on hand for prompt response: Aquarium salt
   Water conditioner

Test kits (ammonia, nitrite, nitrate, pH) Broad-spectrum antibiotic
   Antifungal and antiparasitic treatments

Quarantine tank setup (5–10 gallons) Medicated food or antibacterial fish
food
   Conclusion: Healthy Fish Are Happy Fish
   While goldfish are generally hardy, they are not immune to illness—
especially in cramped or dirty environments. Vigilance, cleanliness, and
an understanding of common ailments will prepare you to handle health
concerns confidently. By responding early and maintaining optimal tank
conditions, you ensure your goldfish enjoy long, vibrant lives.

Chapter 16

Goldfish Breeding at Home: Techniques and Tips

B reeding goldfish at home is an exciting and rewarding endeavor. It allows keepers to witness the complete lifecycle of their fish, preserve specific traits, and contribute to the lineage of beautiful specimens. However, successful goldfish breeding requires patience, preparation, and careful observation.

1. Understanding Goldfish Breeding Behavior

Goldfish are egg layers and do not provide parental care. Their breeding is generally seasonal in the wild, triggered by changes in water temperature and daylight. In captivity, these cues can be artificially mimicked.

Sexual Maturity
Goldfish typically become sexually mature between 1–2 years of age.

Males tend to be slimmer and develop breeding tubercles (tiny white bumps) on their gill covers and pectoral fins during spawning season.
Females are rounder, especially when full of eggs. Spawning Behavior
Males chase females vigorously, nudging their abdomens to stimulate egg release.

This can last several hours and often results in eggs being scattered across surfaces like plants and tank walls.

1. Preparing for Breeding
2. Breeding Tank Setup Tank Size: 20–40 gallons.

Substrate: Bare-bottom or fine gravel (easier to clean).

Decor: Include spawning mops, fine-leaved plants, or breeding brushes for eggs to adhere to.

Water Conditions:

Temperature: 65°F to 75°F. pH: 7.0–7.4.
    Gentle filtration with low current.

1. Conditioning the Breeders

Feed males and females high-quality, protein-rich foods (bloodworms, brine shrimp, daphnia) for 2–3 weeks.

Separate sexes during this time to stimulate desire to breed.

1. Spawning Trigger

Gradually increase water temperature (about 2°F per day) up to 75°F. Increase daylight exposure to simulate spring.
    Reintroduce males and females into the breeding tank.

1. Spawning and Egg Care Spawning Process

Once spawning begins, the female releases hundreds to thousands of eggs. The male simultaneously fertilizes them.

Eggs stick to surfaces and hatch within 4–7 days, depending on temperature.

Important: Remove Parents Goldfish will eat their own eggs.

Remove adults immediately after spawning to prevent loss of fertilized eggs. Fertilized vs. Unfertilized Eggs

Fertilized: Clear with a visible dot (embryo).

Unfertilized: Cloudy or white — these should be removed to prevent fungus.

1. Caring for the Fry Hatching and Early Days

Fry hatch within a week and stick to surfaces for the first day or two. They begin free-swimming and require food shortly afterward.

Feeding Fry

First foods: Infusoria, liquid fry food, or newly hatched baby brine shrimp. Gradually introduce crushed flakes or powdered goldfish food after a week.

Water Quality

Perform small daily water changes.

Maintain stable temperature and gentle filtration (sponge filters are ideal). Growth and Separation

As fry grow, sort them by size to prevent cannibalism.

Move them into larger tanks as needed to support healthy growth.

1. Selective Breeding Tips

If your goal is to develop specific traits (e.g., color, tail type, body shape): Choose compatible pairs that exhibit desired characteristics.

Cull weak or deformed fry early to focus resources on strong specimens. Maintain detailed records of parentage and outcomes.

Be patient—refining a line may take multiple generations.

1. Ethical Considerations

Only breed if you can house, care for, or rehome the resulting fry. Avoid inbreeding, which leads to genetic defects.

Prevent overpopulation by planning carefully.

Conclusion: A Joyful Milestone in Goldfish Keeping

Breeding goldfish at home offers a deeper connection to your fish and opens a window into nature's lifecycle. While it demands attention and care, the reward of raising healthy goldfish from egg to adult is unparalleled. By following sound breeding practices, you'll not only preserve the beauty of your fish but also enhance your appreciation for their complexity.

Chapter 17

Seasonal Care and Temperature Management

G oldfish are hardy creatures capable of adapting to a range of environmental conditions, but as temperatures fluctuate throughout the year, their needs can change dramatically. Proper seasonal care and temperature management are essential to ensuring their long-term health, especially for those kept in outdoor ponds or homes with unregulated climates.

1. Understanding Goldfish Temperature Tolerance

Goldfish are cold-water fish, thriving in temperatures between 65°F and 75°F (18°C–24°C). However, they can survive in temperatures as low as 50°F (10°C) and as high as 80°F (27°C) for short periods. Beyond these limits, their health begins to deteriorate.

Key Points:
Rapid temperature changes are more dangerous than extremes. Drastic fluctuations stress the immune system and can lead to illness.
Monitor water temperatures with a reliable aquarium thermometer year-round.

1. Spring Care: Awakening from Dormancy

Spring is the time goldfish become more active after the winter chill, especially in outdoor ponds.

What to Do:
   Gradually resume feeding once temperatures consistently exceed 50°F (10°C). Begin with easily digestible foods, such as wheat germ pellets.
   Perform a partial water change to remove debris accumulated over winter. Test water parameters as biological activity resumes.
   Inspect for any injuries or infections that may have developed during dormancy.

1. Summer Care: Managing Heat and Oxygen Levels

Summer can pose challenges, especially when temperatures rise above 75°F (24°C). Warm water holds less dissolved oxygen, which goldfish need to breathe.

Tips:
   Increase aeration with air stones, bubbler wands, or waterfalls. Use a fan or aquarium chiller if your tank or pond overheats.
   Avoid overcrowding—more fish = more oxygen demand.

Feed lighter portions and avoid feeding during the hottest part of the day. Provide shaded areas in outdoor ponds using water lilies or artificial covers.

1. Fall Care: Preparing for Winter

Fall is the season of transition. As water temperatures begin to drop, goldfish gradually enter a slower metabolic state.

What to Do:

Begin feeding high-fiber, low-protein foods to prepare their digestive system. Clean the tank or pond to remove fallen leaves and organic matter.

Slowly reduce feeding frequency as temperatures drop below 60°F (15°C).

Stop feeding entirely when water falls below 50°F (10°C), as goldfish cannot digest food properly at these temperatures.

1. Winter Care: Supporting Dormancy

In colder climates, goldfish in outdoor ponds enter a dormant state during winter. Indoor goldfish may not enter full dormancy but will become less active.

Outdoor Ponds:

Ensure the pond is deep enough (at least 2–3 feet) to prevent freezing solid. Use a floating de-icer or pond heater to keep a hole in the ice for gas exchange.

Avoid disturbing the fish or performing water changes during freezing temperatures. Do not feed during dormancy.

Indoor Aquariums:

Keep temperature stable with a heater (if needed) or by insulating the tank. Reduce lighting duration to mimic natural winter conditions.

Monitor for diseases, as immune response is lower in colder months.

1. Year-Round Temperature Stability Tips

Aquarium heaters: Essential for maintaining stable temperatures in cold homes. Aquarium chillers or fans: Useful during hot summer days.

Insulation: Styrofoam or insulating wraps can buffer tanks from ambient temperature shifts. Consistent monitoring: Use digital thermometers and temperature alarms for peace of mind.

Conclusion: Planning with the Seasons

Caring for goldfish is not a static responsibility—it requires adapting to nature's rhythm. With mindful adjustments and seasonal planning, you can ensure your goldfish remain comfortable and healthy no matter the time of year. Whether you keep them indoors or out, your attentiveness to their seasonal needs will reward you with vibrant, thriving fish all year round.

Chapter 18

The Joy and Benefits of Goldfish Keeping

G oldfish keeping is far more than a hobby—it's an enriching and elegant experience that brings beauty, calm, and learning into your home. Whether you're just starting out or have nurtured goldfish for years, the rewards of this endeavor are profound and lasting.

1. A Living Work of Art

Goldfish, with their flowing fins and vivid colors, are like moving art. Watching them swim gracefully through a well-maintained tank or tranquil pond creates a mesmerizing visual experience. The play of light on their scales, the slow undulation of their fins, and their gentle interactions can transform any space into a peaceful, living display.

Aesthetic enhancement: Goldfish tanks can become the centerpiece of a room. Mood lighting: Soft illumination from aquariums adds warmth and elegance.

1. Therapeutic and Stress-Relieving

Numerous studies have shown that observing fish in an aquarium can lower stress levels, reduce anxiety, and even stabilize blood pressure. This is particularly helpful in today's fast-paced world where mental wellness is essential.

Mindfulness: Watching fish swim encourages slow, deliberate observation. Routine care: Feeding and cleaning schedules offer grounding and structure. Relaxation: Aquariums can have a calming, almost meditative effect.

1. An Educational Experience

Goldfish keeping provides valuable educational opportunities for children and adults alike. It promotes responsibility, patience, problem-solving, and basic understanding of biology and environmental balance.

Science in action: Learn about water chemistry, filtration, nutrition, and life cycles. Family activity: Caring for fish can become a shared learning project for households.

Behavior observation: Goldfish are more intelligent than many expect— recognizing feeding times, learning to interact with humans, and even showing unique personalities.

1. A Connection with Nature

Keeping goldfish bridges the gap between urban living and the natural world. The act of nurturing life in an aquarium or pond fosters a greater appreciation for aquatic ecosystems and biodiversity.

Seasonal awareness: Observing changes in fish behavior as seasons shift deepens environmental understanding.

Eco-consciousness: Proper care includes minimizing waste and maintaining balanced habitats.

1. Personal Growth and Fulfillment

The journey of caring for goldfish—from setting up a tank to maintaining a thriving aquatic community—can bring a sense of purpose and satisfaction. The challenges and triumphs that come with goldfish keeping can help build perseverance, compassion, and pride in one's accomplishments.

Goal setting: Whether it's breeding, aquascaping, or perfecting water quality, goals provide motivation.

Art and creativity: Designing aquariums blends science with personal expression. Legacy: Some fishkeepers pass on their love of goldfish to future generations.

1. Community and Shared Passion

There is a vibrant community of goldfish keepers around the world. Whether online or in local clubs, connecting with others who share your interest adds another rewarding dimension.

Forums and groups: Exchange advice, share photos, and ask questions.

Competitions and shows: Many enthusiasts take part in goldfish exhibitions and breed shows.
Mentorship: Experienced hobbyists often guide newcomers, fostering camaraderie. Final Thoughts: A Lasting Bond
Caring for goldfish is about more than just feeding and cleaning. It's about forming a bond
with living creatures and taking pride in creating a stable, beautiful environment for them to thrive. Their subtle elegance, resilience, and timeless charm are what make them such beloved companions across cultures and generations.

Whether you've chosen a single elegant comet or a whole community of fanciful varieties, your dedication to their care is what brings them to life—not just as fish, but as cherished members of your household.

Congratulations! You've reached the end of the Goldfish Home Keeping Handbook. With the knowledge you now possess, you're well-prepared to embark on or continue your journey into the elegant world of goldfish care—with confidence, creativity, and joy.

Printed in Dunstable, United Kingdom

70859939R00051